GUINEA PIG SOLO

inspired by Büchner's
WOYZECK

Brett C Leonard

BROADWAY PLAY PUBLISHING INC
New York
www.broadwayplaypublishing.com
info@broadwayplaypublishing.com

GUINEA PIG SOLO
© Copyright 2010 by Brett C Leonard

Cover photo by Carol Rosegg
First printing: October 2010
I S B N: 978-0-88145-458-1

Book design: Marie Donovan
Typographic controls: Adobe InDesign
Typeface: Palatino
Printed and bound in the U S A

GUINEA PIG SOLO was first performed in December 2003 at the Public Theater in New York City as part of LAByrinth Theater Company's annual Barn Series. The cast and creative contributor were:

JOSE .... John Ortiz
VIVIAN ....Elizabeth Rodriguez
GARY/BICYCLE COP .... Stephen Adly Guirgis
CHARLIE SANSONE .... Richard Petrocelli
NIKKI/RECEPTIONIST .... Colleen Werthmann
ZOO GUIDE .... Florencia Lozano
JOHN RODRIGUEZ .... David Zayas
DOCTOR KRAMER .... Bob Glaudini
JUNIOR .... Carlo Alban

Director ....Ian Belton

The world premiere of GUINEA PIG SOLO was on 20 April 2004 at the Public Theater (George C Wolfe, Artistic Director) in New York City in a co-production with LAByrinth Theater Company (Philip Seymour Hoffman and John Ortiz, Artistic Directors). The cast and creative contributor were:

JOSE	John Ortiz
VIVIAN	Judy Reyes
GARY/BICYCLE COP	Stephen Adly Guirgis
CHARLIE SANSONE	Richard Petrocelli
NIKKI/RECEPTIONIST	Portia
ZOO GUIDE	Kim Director
JOHN RODRIGUEZ	Jason Manuel Olazabal
DOCTOR KRAMER	Bob Glaudini
JUNIOR	Alex Flores
Director	Ian Belton
Set design	Andromache Chalfant
Costume design	Kaye Voyce
Lighting design	Paul Whitaker
Sound design	Fitz Patton

CHARACTERS

Jose
Receptionist
Bicycle Cop
Charlie Sansone
Vivian
Gary
Junior
Nurses
John Rodriguez
Doctor Kramer
Nikki
Zoo Guide
Scientists

New York City

for Elizabeth

Scene 1

(Food Stand on New York City Sidewalk)

(JOSE SOLO tries to make a sale.)

JOSE: I got hot dogs.
I got muffins.
I got coffee.
I got donuts.
I got mustard.
I got ketchup.
I got candy bars.
I got nutrasweet.
Come on people.
Step right up, people.
Step right up people. Buy something people. Buy yourself a hot dog.

Scene 2

(A barber shop)

(JOSE, wearing a white barber's coat, sits in a barber's chair—a pair of scissors in his hand.)

Scene 3

(A pay phone)

(JOSE inserts a quarter and dials a number. He waits. And waits. And waits.)

(He hangs up.)

Scene 4

(JOSE runs in place.)

JOSE: Love and be loved
Love and be loved
To love and be loved
Love and be loved
To love and be loved
Love and be loved
To love and be loved
Love and be loved...

Scene 5

(Food stand)

JOSE: I got sauerkraut and onions. I got Snickers and Milkyways. I got caffeine and decaf. I got blueberry muffins. I got zucchini muffins. I got poppyseed muffins. I got cranberry muffins. I got soft shell crab. I got giant prawns. I got Kung Pao chicken. I got lamb kabab. I got falafel. I got stuffed mushrooms. I got Belgian waffles with fresh strawberries. I got fettucini alfredo. I got cannolies with fruit in 'em. I got a lotta shit here people. Step right up, people. Buy something, people. Buy something.

Scene 6

(V A hospital waiting room)

JOSE: I had a ten-thirty appointment.

RECEPTIONIST: Jose Solo, yes, we have you down for a ten-thirty with Doctor Kramer.

JOSE: And now it's noon.

RECEPTIONIST: Creeping up on it, yes, any minute now.

JOSE: I've been here for an hour and a half.

RECEPTIONIST: We'll call your name when we're ready.

JOSE: Do you have any idea when that might be?

RECEPTIONIST: I answer phones, I don't predict the future.

JOSE: I've been here for an hour and a half.

RECEPTIONIST: I understand your frustration, sir.

JOSE: You do NOT understand my frustration.

RECEPTIONIST: I'm a strong observer of human behavior.

JOSE: I need to see Doctor Kramer and I've been here for an hour and a half and all I've done—all I've done in that hour and a half is filled out paperwork.

RECEPTIONIST: That paperwork is extremely important for your file, sir.

JOSE: I had to leave my job ta get here. To keep the appointment I made—the appointment YOU made—the time YOU GAVE ME—and I'm here—I made good on my end—and I ain't doin' so good right now, okay? So—look—what I need to know is...when will I be able to see my fuckin' doctor?!

Scene 7

(Pay phone)

(JOSE, receiver in hand, waits. And waits. And waits.)

JOSE: C'mon. Answer. Answer. Answer. Answer the fuckin' phone!! *(He slams the receiver against its cradle.)*

Scene 8

(Barber shop)

(JOSE, in the chair, opens and closes and opens and closes and opens and closes the scissors.)

Scene 9

(JOSE, center stage, runs in place.)

JOSE: ...and love you and love me
and kiss you and kiss me
and miss you and miss me
and fuck you and fuck me
and love you and love me
and haircuts and hotdogs and murder
and love and intestines and love and family and love
and love and love and love and love and love and love
and love...

Scene 10

(V A hospital)

(JOSE stands across from DR. KRAMER—fifties—male.

JOSE: I gotta see more a' you than I been seein' -- I'm ready ta do what you told me—I'm ready for the tests—I'm ready for the experiments—I need the money—when can I see you? I gotta get back ta my jobs— I'm ready, Doctor. When can we begin?

Scene 11

(Food stand)

(A BICYCLE COP *is writing a ticket in front of the abandoned food stand.)*

*(*JOSE *enters running.)*

JOSE: Whoa, whoa, whoa, whoa, whoa—excuse me, officer, I , uh...I just hadda run to the bathroom real quick. I'm back now.

BICYCLE COP: You do realize it's a violation to leave your cart unattended.

JOSE: I just hadda go ta the bathroom real quick.

BICYCLE COP: An unattended cart is an unattended cart.

JOSE: I know, I just—c'mon man—I just hadda take a little leak, that's all—c'mon—Guy ta guy. Whaddaya say?

BICYCLE COP: Don't blame me. Blame Bloomberg.

(The BICYCLE COP *holds out the ticket.* JOSE *doesn't take it.)*

JOSE: You ride a bicycle.

BICYCLE COP: Take the ticket, sir.

JOSE: You wear shorts and you ride a bicycle and you carry a gun and you write fuckin' tickets.

BICYCLE COP: And you work at a food stand.

(The BICYCLE COP *tries to put the ticket on* JOSE's *food stand.* JOSE *grabs the* BICYCLE COP's *hand, yanks it up behind his back, and slams his face against the food stand while:)*

JOSE: MOTHERFUCKER! You shouldn't be allowed to wear a uniform—fuckin' bitch!!!

(CRACK! Police officer CHARLIE SANSONE, *fifties, whacks the butt of his gun against* JOSE's *temple.)*

(Blackout)

Scene 12

(In black)

*(We hear a woman's [*VIVIAN's*] voice.)*

VIVIAN: And then the three of us can crawl into bed together—and we can rent old black and white movies and order Chinese food or pizza for delivery. Not the black and white movies with Humphrey Bogart or James Cagney with all the violence in them—but something nice for Junior to see. What's the one about Santa Claus and the little girl where nobody really believes he's Santa Claus except for her? That would be a good one for us to watch. It's a good movie. It's about believing in things even when everybody else tries to make it so you don't believe in them. If you believe hard enough in something, there is no such thing as hoping against hope. It's like love. If you believe in it hard enough—no matter what might happen or what people might think about it -- love lasts forever if you want it to. At least that's what I believe anyway. I love you Vivian. I love you, too Junior. I can't wait to see you both soon. You are the reasons why I try to stay alive.

Scene 13

(New York City sidewalk)

(CHARLIE is sitting on the curb, smoking a cigarette.)

(JOSE is unconscious on the ground.)

(The food stand has been taken away.)

(JOSE stirs awake.)

CHARLIE: Been out awhile, kid.

(Beat)

(JOSE sits up.)

CHARLIE: Wan' a smoke?

(CHARLIE holds out a cigarette. JOSE takes it. CHARLIE strikes a match and lights JOSE's smoke.)

CHARLIE: Your boss came by while you were takin' your snooze. Your supervisor, somebody. Couldn't save your job, kid. Put in a good word for ya, but... ya know...all splayed out on the concrete like that... didn't look too good for business. Whaddaya gonna do? *(Pause)* Ya know...you chose losin' your job—and riskin' goin' ta jail—rather than payin' a goddamn fine. Wear an orange jumpsuit. Be told when ta wake. When ta sleep. When ta take a shit. Get a tattoo of a naked woman on your back, givin' Leroy and Rufus some'n nice ta gaze on they're poundin' ya fulla black cock. 'Steada payin' a ticket. Not a lotta sense in my book. Not a lot goin' on upstairs. Too much emotion, not enough thought. The emotions? The fisticuffs? That don't make for a very easy life. Ya understand? What's your name, son? Go on. I'm Charlie—who'm I talkin' to?

JOSE: Jose.

CHARLIE: Jose. *(Beat)* I did two tours, Jose. Sixty-seven ta sixty-nine. *(Beat)* Your arm.

(JOSE *pulls his shirt sleeve down over his military tattoo.*)

CHARLIE: Made some friends, lost some friends. Give an' take. Ya understand? Give an' take, up an' down. This is life. The good, the bad—the in-between. Made me the man I am today. Ya understand? At's alright. Maybe someday you will. *(Beat)* I'm gonna keep an eye on you. The officer you assaulted? He wanted ta drag your ass inta the cage. I told'm do his job. Told'm I'd take care a' you. So don't go makin' me an asshole on this. Ya step outta line? Ya fuck up again on my streets? I'm gonna drag your ass in myself. Take ya in the backroom, shove a plunger up your ass. Ya understand? I'm givin' you a second chance here. *(Beat)* You can thank me if you want.

JOSE: Thanks.

CHARLIE: You're welcome. *(He holds out the ticket.)* Now take the ticket. Go on. Take the ticket. Ya take the ticket, ya pay the fine—you'll feel better about the whole goddamn thing. Go on. What's right is right.

(JOSE *takes the ticket.*)

CHARLIE: You gonna be able ta make good on this? You got another job ta help ya out? Construction, some'n like that?

JOSE: I cut hair.

CHARLIE: Excuse me?

JOSE: I cut people's hair.

CHARLIE: You're homosexual.

JOSE: No, I...

CHARLIE: ...no, no, don't ask, don't tell, right? No matter how wrong it might be. Ya know my day, we'd ask— they'd tell—we didn't like what we heard—crack ta the skull with the butt of a rifle. It's a different time nowadays. Whaddaya gonna do? It's a different time.

(CHARLIE *and* JOSE *sit in silence, side by side.*)

Scene 14

(A Bar)

*(*JOSE *is with his friend* GARY.*)*

JOSE: Lookit these motherfuckers—Drunk an' bleary eyed it's three o'clock in the afternoon. C'mon lemme get a smoke, I'm all out.

GARY: You're always all out.

JOSE: Juss gimme a fuckin' cigarette will ya? Wha' do I owe you—thirty cents? I'll give ya the thirty cents.

*(*GARY *gives* JOSE *a cigarette.*)*

GARY: Ya owe me thirty cents—an' I don't want no fuckin' pennies, either.

JOSE: Only fuckin' bar still lets us smoke, some prick'll prolly waltz in here start writin' shit up. They leave the suits alone who can AFFORD the fine—come bustin' our balls instead. That's the way shit works.

GARY: That's the way shit works.

JOSE: Take a shit on the little guy, wipe the big guy's ass. That's the shit we're up against us, bro.

GARY: Up against it, up against it. It's us against the world, Jose. Why do we even get outta bed in the morning?

JOSE: This shit's funny to you? Mmmph? You find this shit to be funny?

GARY: NOTHING is funny to you.

JOSE: No, plenty a' shit's funny ta me—I happen to have a very good sense a' humor—but gettin' fucked in the ass three times a day? Not a lotta laughs, bro, believe me.

GARY: You got a ticket, Jose.

JOSE: Hundred twenny five motherfuckin' dollar ticket, that's right! And for what? Mmmph? For what? For leavin' a dirty bomb in the airport? For a FOOD cart on a SIDEWALK. A food cart, Gary—it had hot dogs in it.

GARY: You got a ticket, Jose—you didn't get fucked in the ass.

JOSE: Yeah, well...you got your theories, I got mine.

GARY: I ain't got as many as you do, bro.

JOSE: Yeah, well, maybe you should.

GARY: Seein' how it works wonders for you, right?

JOSE: Whatever, bro.

GARY: Whatever.

JOSE: Whatever.

GARY: Whatever.

JOSE: Mothafucker fires me. FIRES me. For bein' IRRESPONSIBLE. [Irresponsible.] Fuck I suppose ta do? Irresponsible. Fuckin' cop, fuckin' boss, fuckin' ticket. Fuckin' life, bro. So I don't go ta jail, so what? Don't gotta pay no rent in jail. Buy groceries, pay bills—none a that shit. Makin' license plates? Who gives a shit? What I got now? Huh? What I got now? Cuttin' hair, pickin bread crumbs outta fat motherfuckers' beards. Two customers a day. Lookit these mothafuckers—sad-ass drinkin' three o' clock the afternoon in this bullshit. Got nowhere else ta go. Nothin' ta do. Landlord's with the eviction notice. Loved ones are dead. Or left 'em. What else they supposed ta do? Huh? Go out dancin'? Ride the merry-go-round Coney Island? This is the world, bro. This the world God gave us. A world a' jock itch an' heart disease—and don't forget to smile. Don't forget ta get down on your knees and give the Lord Jesus Christ

Our Savior a great big thanks—big ass thanks. Amen,
God bless, Nina, Pinta, Santa Maria, and fuck you, too.
Have a good life bitches. Go on. Enjoy yourself.

GARY: You gotta try an' learn not ta think so much, bro.

JOSE: Try ta learn not ta think so much?

GARY: You know—just...ya gotta try ta learn ta think a'
nothin' every once in a while.

JOSE: Think a' nothin'?

GARY: Yeah, just—you know—learn ta think a' nothin'
when you can.

JOSE: LEARN ta THINK of NOTHING?

GARY: Have a conversation every once in a while. 'Bout
the Yankees, whatever.

JOSE: I'm a Mets fan.

GARY: Whatever, bro—talk about the weather every
once in a while—it's gonna be a cloudy day, a sunny
day, fuckin tornado, whatever—some'n just not so
goddamn important all the time.

JOSE: You wanna talk about the weather?

GARY: The weather, what you had for breakfast this
morning—it don't matter, just...

JOSE: ...I got fucked in the ass for breakfast this
morning—wha'd you have?

GARY: I had a bowl a' Honeynut Cheerios. And a nice
refreshing, ice cold glass of orange juice. That shit was
delicious, bro.

JOSE: This is who I'm havin' a conversation with.

GARY: A conversation, yes—two people sittin' around
talking.

JOSE: Talkin' bullshit is what we're sittin' around talkin'. "Learn ta not try an' think so much. Think a' nothin'."

GARY: Nothin' important, is what I'm sayin'. Quick— think of an elephant.

JOSE: What're you talkin' about?

GARY: You're thinkin' of an elephant right now, aren't you?

JOSE: I'm not thinkin' of an elephant.

GARY: You fuckin' haveta be—it's a scientific fact.

JOSE: Well, I'm not, so...

GARY: ...How much you wanna bet right now—right this very second—after I say the word "elephant"— you're gonna be thinkin' of an elephant?

JOSE: How 'bout the thirty cents for the cigarette?

GARY: ELEPHANT!

JOSE: I'm not thinkin' a' one—we're even.

GARY: Bullshit—you ARE thinkin' a one—you can say you're not, but you fuckin' are—you haveta be—it's a proven scientific fact.

JOSE: What is?

GARY: TO THINK OF AN ELEPHANT WHEN I SAY ELEPHANT. It's been proven. "Elephant." Go on— what're you thinkin' about?

JOSE: I'm thinkin' about the fuckin' idiot I'm sittin' next to.

GARY: C'mon, man—admit it—elephants, rats—what difference does it make? It's called conversation, bro. Which, by the way you shoulda seen this shit I seen on T V about drowning rats, bro—earlier today—when you were out gettin' fired—I'm tellin' ya—that shit was extremely INTERESTING.

JOSE: How come I have absolutely no idea what the fuck you're talking about?

GARY: I'm talkin' about this documentary shit I seen on T V today where they was drowning' rats an' shit—very interesting stuff. See—they'd put these rats in these buckets a' water, right...

JOSE: ...What the fuck're you talkin' about? Elephants, rats, caterpillars—who gives a shit? What the hell are you talkin' about?

GARY: Yeah, right—Steada what you wanna talk about, right? "The world, Gary, the world."

JOSE: The world God gave us, that's right.

GARY: If God gave us the world, he musta given us the rats, too.

JOSE: So what?

GARY: So what difference does it make?

JOSE: What difference does what make?

GARY: What we talk about? What difference does it make?

JOSE: Cuz maybe I'm not interested in talkin' about rats.

GARY: Why not?

JOSE: Because I find them to be uninteresting.

GARY: But you don't even know what I was gonna say about 'em.

JOSE: I don't have to know—they don't interest me.

GARY: Yeah, but if you seen the shit on T V. I seen...

JOSE: ...I woulda changed the fuckin' channel.

GARY: Ya see, that's exactly what I'm talkin' about about you. Some people would consider that ta be very close minded of you.

JOSE: Some people can lick my ass.

GARY: Ya know, you accuse everybody else a' bein' close minded, but somehow it don't matter when it's you who's the one doin' the shit.

JOSE: You're tellin' me about somebody, somewhere, drowning fuckin' rats. I don't give a shit about somebody drowning rats. Drown away—what am I— best friend a' the fuckin' rat!?

GARY: You know what, bro...

JOSE: ...what?...

GARY: ...whenever you wanna talk about something I let you talk on and on—but if YOU don't wanna talk about some shit I may wanna talk about, I'm not allowed to. Now that's fuckin' bullshit. You're allowed to an' I'm not—very upsetting, bro.

JOSE: You're upset over this?

GARY: I'd say I'm hurt a little, yeah.

JOSE: Alright—look—you're allowed ta talk about whatever the fuck you wanna talk about, alright?

GARY: Long as it ain't elephants or rats or...

JOSE: ...No, bro, no—talk about whatever the fuck you wanna talk about—just leave my shit out of it, okay?

GARY: You ain't gettin' no more cigarettes, bro. Fuckin' done with that shit.

JOSE: Gary?

GARY: What?

JOSE: I don't give a shit about rats. I don't give a shit about elephants. I don't give a fuck about giraffes or turtles, zebras, two-headed snakes, or the hump- backed motherfuckin' whale! I don't—fuckin'—care about that shit! I got bigger fish ta fry, ya understand? Bigger fish.

GARY: You know why the salmons swim upstream?

JOSE: I DON'T GIVE A SHIT WHY SALMON SWIM
UPSTREAM! Jesus-fuckin'-Christ!! YOU can talk about
bullshit! You can try ta learn ta think of nothing if
that's what you wanna do- just leave my shit out of it,
okay? LEARN TA THINK OF NOTHING—shit don't
even make any goddamn sense! Ya learn something—
you learn SOME-THING! Not NO-THING! SOME-
THING. You learn SOME-THING- fuckin' shit, bro!
It's no way ta go through life thinkin' that shit, learnin'
nothin', talkin' bullshit twenny-four seven. We are
what we are— An' ya know what? We don't stand
a chance, guys like you an' me--deck stacked up
against us an' all that shit. The doctor with the welfare
moms? The dentist from Bed-Stuy? I don't know those
mothafuckers—you know those mothafuckers? How
many Colin Powells we grow up playin' dodgeball
with? Bullshit. Your father—he doin' twenny-five
ta life he ran a little weed tryin' ta put food on the
table, your moms is walkin' dead bustin' her ass
sixteen-eighteen hours a day cleanin' toilets a some
silver-spoon bullshit- ya gettin' your ass ahead goin'
through it that way? Ivy League diploma on your
motherfuckin' wall next ta the crucifix an' the busted-
up cockroach legs? Fuck that! Not in this world OR the
next- if there even is a next- an' what is it you think
about that shit? Huh? Whaddayou think? There's a
heaven, there's a God? Look around your ass- look out
your window someday, ridin' subways, lookin' at the
faces standin', sittin' all around you. If we're created
in God's image, that's one sad, long-faced all-powerful
motherfucker. Shoulda made us in somebody else's
image. Rich motherfucker's image. Rolex watches,
penthouse apartments, cars an' private drivers- they
piss on guys like you an' me. In their eyes they shit on
us. We're on welfare an' food stamps an' park benches

with newspaper blankets, pissin' our pants, panting
for their daughters with eyes buggin' out our fuckin'
heads- sittin' on the stoop drinkin' forties, taggin' their
precious city-owned overpriced walls. Fuck George
Senior! And George W too! Dick Cheney—all them
mothafuckers. Mayor Mike Bloomberg? Fuck him too.
I wanna cigarette I'll smoke it wherever the fuck I feel
like smokin' it. "An unattended cart is an unattended
cart." "Don't blame me, blame Bloomberg." I blame all
y'all mothafuckers. Thumbin' their coke-filled noses
at guys like you an' me- howlin' at the moon- playin'
with our switchblades- dirty Porta Rican spick-ass
motherfuckers-messin' with their fire hydrants,
wilding in the park. It's two hundred thirty seven
degrees out, got no air condition', got no Super ta fix
'em when we do got 'em—you goddamn right I'm
fuckin' with the hydrants. I'll sit smack dead middle
a that shit NAKED—water shootin' straight up my
sweet brown Puerto Rican ass. I'll put a mothafuckin'
MILK CRATE on top of the fuckin' hydrant, sit on that
shit, smoke me a mothafuckin' Newport while I'm at
it! Fuck dem bitches! N Y P D. U S M C. They can all
tongue my piss-hole all I care. It's our lot in LIFE- it'll
be our lot in mothafuckin' DEATH. Be put ta work in
Heaven if we're lucky enough ta get there in the first
place. All of us—every last one—poor motherfuckers?
You don't got no cash? Ain't put away 'nuff greenbacks
your ass was on the earth? Get over there, bitches, get
in the I-don't-got-no-motherfuckin' money line up in
Heaven. Or the English-is-my-second-language line.
Or the your-skin-ain't-quite-white enough line—fuck
you—all a you—over there against the wall, hands
up an' spread 'em, this shit mothafuckin' shake down
time. Be on Heaven's assembly line pullin' down
minimum-fuckin'—I work at Burger King wages—
makin' thunder an' lightnin' for niggas still livin' down
below. An' other mothafuckers up there with us? Rich,

white mothafuckers, got their hands in Wall Street?
Got their hands in oil down in Texas? Be havin' orgies
an' chill-ass Grey Goose apple flavor martinis, kickin'
with slot machines an' lucky sevens, filet mignons an'
French shit I can't even pronounce. Not us, bro. To the
assembly lines. It's nine-eleven, an' December seven,
an' the fourth of motherfuckin' July 1776. September
eleven mighta woke up some niggas but it didn't
wake up enough a them still sound sleepin' countin'
sheep motherfuckers. Sleepin' hard. Sleepin' deep, bro.
Smilin', peaceful, wakin' up in wet dreams an' silk
sheets—I'm Afganistan! Operation Iraqi Occupation!
Vietnam! I'm the mothafuckin' beaches a Normandy!
I waved my motherfuckin' flag. I was over there while
bitches sat on their fat Twinkie eatin' asses tunin' in
on motherfuckin' C N N, wishin' us well, wishin' us
safe return. Blood and oil on my body, my clothes,
my hair—in my motherfuckin' eyes—holding a three
year old Iraqi girl's intestines in my hands, tryin'
ta resuscitate her she's already fuckin' dead. Her
intestines in my hands. Go over there and kill, soldier.
Go over there an' try ta stay alive so I can profit from
your insanity. Make me rich, soldier, make me richer
than I already am. Pat on the back, thank you for your
troubles, good luck at the food stand, best a' luck at
the barber shop. What's with the long face, soldier?
Ya did good, soldier, put a smile on your face, soldier,
walk proud, soldier, stand tall—and by the way—oh
yeah—welcome back, soldier—welcome home—sure
is glad ya didn't catch one in the gut while you were
there, happy ya didn't get one to the head—sorry
'bout your buddies Tommy an' Luke an' Justin an'
lil' Frankie—sorry they didn't make it, but yeah, boy,
yessir, we sure is glad ta see you doin' alright—how
about a ribbon? Would ya like a ribbon, soldier? How
'bout a medal or two you can wear while you're out
sellin' hot dogs an' lemonade? Tha'd be nice, donchya

think? Every second, every day they bleed me of my
life, of my wife, of my child, of who I am myself. That
which does not kill me makes me wanna kill somebody
else. Kill or be killed? Love and be loved. To love and
be loved—nothing else—nothing. Everything else is
fuckin' bullshit—dogshit—catshit. Love and be loved.
Or eat a dick. *(Beat)* I'm lyin'? Mmmph? I'm lyin'?
(Beat) C'mon—lemme get another cigarette. I'm gonna
be late for my RE-SCHEDULED appointment.

GARY: Ya know what, Jose?

JOSE: What?

GARY: You really gotta learn ta not think so much.

Scene 15

(VIVIAN's apartment)

(VIVIAN smokes at the kitchen table.)

*(Ten-year-old JUNIOR is on the floor bouncing a small, blue,
rubber ball against a wall.)*

*(From a small portable radio we hear Sammy Davis Jr.
singing* Blame It On My Youth.*)*

(When the song ends we hear:)

D J: *(V O)* That was Sammy Davis Jr. with the Marty
Paich Orchestra doing their rendition of *Blame It On My
Youth* for Warner Reprise on the *Wham of Sam* record.
Next up's the original King. This is Nat King Cole and
Those Lazy Hazy Crazy Days of Summer, Capitol Records,
1963.

(Nat King Cole sings.)

(Blackout)

Scene 16

(V A hospital)

(JOSE runs on a treadmill. He is hooked up to tubes in his nose, needles in his arms, E K G suction cups on his shirtless torso. A monitor beeps and flashes. Two NURSES check and record his vital signs.)

(DOCTOR KRAMER holds up one Rorschach card after another.)

JOSE: The wing of a 757. The soul of a kamikaze. 27,000 grains of sand. A camel with three humps. A baby with no limbs. Olives and pita bread.

DOCTOR KRAMER: Faster.

(The treadmill moves faster and faster.)

JOSE: Tower one. Tower two. My wife. My son.

DOCTOR KRAMER: Faster.

(And even faster still.)

JOSE: My wife. My son. My wife. My son.

DOCTOR KRAMER: Focus!!!

JOSE: Stars and stripes and red and white...

DOCTOR KRAMER: ...Good...

JOSE: ...and black and blue and blood and brains...

DOCTOR KRAMER: ...Focus...

(JOSE can barely hang on.)

JOSE: ...America and murder and hatred and madness...

DOCTOR KRAMER: ...Focus!...

JOSE: ...my wife, my son...

DOCTOR KRAMER: ...Focus!!...

JOSE: ...My wife, my son!!...

(Blackout)

Scene 17

(VIVIAN's *apartment.*)

(VIVIAN *bounces and catches the rubber ball as we saw* JUNIOR *doing earlier.*)

(JUNIOR *smokes at the kitchen table.*)

(*Sammy Davis Jr. is heard singing* Blame It On My Youth. *The song ends.*)

D J: *(V O)*That was Sammy Davis Junior with the Marty Paich Orchestra.

(*Blackout*)

Scene 18

(*V A hospital*)

(JOSE *is seated with a gag in his mouth. Snot pours out of his nose. Tears roll down his face. One* NURSE *records his vital signs. Another* NURSE *administers an intravenous drip.*)

(DOCTOR KRAMER *encourages gently—no fire and brimstone.*)

DOCTOR KRAMER: "Upon the horses, upon the donkeys, upon the camels, upon the herds and flocks: There shall be a very grievous murraine." Exodus 9—Verses 1 through 7. This has been the case for thousands of years. Since the beginning of man, Jose. You're doing great. You're doing terrific.

(*Blackout*)

Scene 19

(VIVIAN's *apartment*)

(VIVIAN *and* JUNIOR *smoke cigarettes at the kitchen table.
They stare straight ahead. Sammy Davis Jr. sings* Blame
It on My Youth. *The telephone is ringing. They pay no
attention. Fifteen seconds.*)

(*Blackout*)

Scene 20

(*V A hospital*)

(JOSE *is in a chair with wires and cables hooked up to his
head, arms and chest. The* NURSES *check his vitals and help
to keep him awake.*)

DOCTOR KRAMER: Seventy-two hours with no sleep is
the goal. Seventy-two hours for two hundred dollars.
An additional two hundred dollars every twenty-four
hours after that. Think of the money, Jose. No. Think of
the future good you are bringing to the world around
you. The future of this great nation will be a wee-bit
brighter for the likes of men like you and me- selfless
men—men who are willing to sacrifice of themselves
for the greater good of mankind. A better tomorrow
for the children of the world. A better tomorrow for
your son. You show me a selfless man, I'll show you a
happy man. Twenty-nine hours and forty-one minutes
remain.

(DOCTOR KRAMER *and the* NURSES *exit.*)

(JOSE *remains in the chair.*)

(*Lights up on* VIVIAN *and* JUNIOR *sitting at their kitchen
table—staring straight ahead. No cigarettes. No ringing
phone. No music*)

(*Silence. Five-ten seconds. Slow fade to black*)

Scene 21

(*Barber Shop.* JOSE *applies shaving cream to* CHARLIE'*s neck and face and begins shaving him with a straight razor.*)

CHARLIE: I like you, Joey. You're alright in my book.

JOSE: It's Jose.

CHARLIE: You're in America now, I call you Joey.

JOSE: Puerto Rico's in America.

CHARLIE: Porta Rica's in the middle a' the fuckin' ocean.

JOSE: Okay.

CHARLIE: Okay. (*Pause*) Your underarms stink, Joey. Your underarms stink an immigrant stink. The stench a' poverty. Your underarms stink the stink a' stupidity. You're all heart an' no brains, Joey. Ya got bags under your eyes the size a' pancakes. Or tortillas probly more appropriate. Your hands are shaking. You breathe like you ran a marathon. You're like a mouse in a glue trap. They don't starve, Joey. There's no poison they eat stuck in the glue. They become frantic. They panic's how they meet their fate. They suffer a series of small heart attacks. Little mouse heart attack after little mouse heart attack until their little mouse hearts finally give out and explode. They die cuz of a lack of patience. Cuz of a lack a trust in their fellow little mouse friends who may be able to save 'em if they weren't in such a goddamn hurry racing for the non-existent finish line. Use your head. Slow down. Count to ten before you speak. Count to a hundred before you act. Now lay the blade against my neck. Gently. The way you'd caress a lover. The way you'd hold a newborn in your arms. Breathe. Relax. Take your time. All heart an' no brains, Joey. That can't make for an easy life. Not a very easy life at all.

Scene 22

(VIVIAN's *apartment*)

(*An empty apartment.* No VIVIAN. No JUNIOR. *No music*)

(*Just a ringing telephone*)

(*Lights up on* JOSE *at a payphone, the receiver to his ear.* Ring. Ring. Ring)

(JOSE *SLAMS and SLAMS and SLAMS and SLAMS the receiver against its cradle.*)

(*Blackout*)

Scene 23

(*Puerto Rican Day Parade*)

(VIVIAN, JUNIOR, *and* NIKKI *smoke cigarettes.*)

NIKKI: What about that one?

VIVIAN: He's all yours.

NIKKI: He's pretty cute.

VIVIAN: (*to* JUNIOR) Okay, so you see those skirt things they're wearing? Those are called "naguas". All married Taino women wore them to cover the lower parts of their bodies. Hundreds of years ago.

NIKKI: I bet Little Boy Blue would love to hear all about it.

VIVIAN: Are you still talking? You're still talking.

NIKKI: I'm talkin' 'bout Little Boy Blue.

VIVIAN: Who the fuck is Little Boy Blue?

NIKKI: Little Boy N Y P D Blue—over there—the one in the mustache.

VIVIAN: Why are you talkin' about him?

NIKKI: He's been staring at you for the last twenty minutes.

VIVIAN: How do you know he hasn't been staring at you?

NIKKI: Cuz I've been tryin' to make eye contact with him but he ain't havin' it.

VIVIAN: So how do you know he's been lookin' at me?

NIKKI: Look at him, he's starin' right at you.

VIVIAN: Which one?

NIKKI: Right there—the cute one.

VIVIAN: I don't see any cute one.

NIKKI: Right there—with the mustache.

VIVIAN: He don't look that cute to me.

NIKKI: Gotta love a man in uniform.

VIVIAN: Depends on the uniform.

NIKKI: Depends on the man. Here he comes, he's walkin' right towards us.

VIVIAN: *(to* JUNIOR*)* Putchyour cigarette out.

*(*VIVIAN *drops and steps on her cigarette. She takes* JUNIOR*'s away, drops it, steps on it.* NIKKI *continues smoking.)*

(Officer JOHN RODRIGUEZ *approaches.)*

JOHN: How are you ladies doing this evening?

VIVIAN: It's ten o'clock in the morning.

JOHN: What's that?

NIKKI: *(Exaggerated)* "How are you ladies doing this EVENING? It's ten o'clock in the MORNING." Get it? She's very funny. Pretty and very, very funny.

VIVIAN: Shut up, Nikki.

NIKKI: Pretty, funny—feisty—she's the whole package, pal. You got your work cut out for you.

JOHN: I enjoy a nice sense of humor.

VIVIAN: I wasn't trying to be funny. I was trying to be rude. I'm sorry.

JOHN: It's okay. Sometimes I can be rude too.

VIVIAN: You asked how we were doing. I'm doing fine. How are you doing?

JOHN: Better—now that I'm talking to you.

NIKKI: Okay, well...I have an appointment I gotta get to, so...

VIVIAN: ...You don't have an appointment.

NIKKI: I DO have an appointment.

JOHN: My shift ends in fifteen minutes...if you'd like me to stay here with you. To protect you. And let your friend make her appointment. I could do that. I could even walk you home, if you like.

VIVIAN: Would you carry my books for me?

JOHN: If you had books to carry.

VIVIAN: I was gonna take Junior to the zoo.

JOHN: I take it you must be Junior.

(JUNIOR *ignores* JOHN.)

VIVIAN: He's my son.

NIKKI: There's no father in the picture, if that's what you were thinking.

VIVIAN: Is that what you were thinking?

JOHN: No. And I happen to love the zoo.

(JOHN *and* VIVIAN *lock eyes. Beat*)

VIVIAN: Say goodbye Nikki. You have an appointment to get to.

NIKKI: I believe I do have an appointment. Goodbye Vivian. Goodbye Junior. And goodbye to you, officer.

(JOHN *takes* NIKKI's *hand.*)

JOHN: My name's John.

(JOHN *kisses* NIKKI's *hand.*)

NIKKI: Gentleman John. Okay, then. Enjoy the zoo.

(NIKKI *walks off.* VIVIAN *and* JOHN *look into each other's eyes.* JUNIOR *continues to stare straight ahead. Pause)*

VIVIAN: Hello, John.

JOHN: Hello.

VIVIAN: I'm Vivian.

JOHN: Hello, Vivian.

VIVIAN: Hello, John.

Scene 24

(V A hospital)

(JOSE *is seated with the gag in his mouth and snot down his nose.)*

DOCTOR KRAMER: How many children did General George S Patton have? Do you know? Jose—do you know? *(Beat)* He had six. Do you know how many children General Eisenhower had? Jose? *(Beat)* He had four children. General Schwarzkopf has three. General Grant had eleven. These were all happily married men. Yet nobody knows how many children they had. These are facts that are very rarely discussed. And do you know why? Jose? Do you know why? *(Beat)* Because nobody cares.

Scene 25

(The Bronx Zoo)

(A picnic table)

(VIVIAN and JOHN drink sodas through straws. JUNIOR stands beside them, eats blue cotton candy and stares at a beautiful female ZOO GUIDE smoking a cigarette on her break.)

JOHN: I'm glad you allowed me to come to the zoo with you, Vivian. I'm having a nice time with you and your son.

VIVIAN: Yeah. It's alright.

JOHN: I would have to say it's better than alright. I would have to say that, uh...that this is kinda nice, actually.

VIVIAN: Yeah. *(Re: JUNIOR staring at the ZOO GUIDE)* Junior seems to be enjoying it too.

Scene 26

(Barber shop)

(JOSE is giving CHARLIE a manicure.)

JOSE: Have you ever been in love, Charlie?

CHARLIE: I've been in love over three hundred times.

JOSE: Nah, I mean love, you know, love, like REAL love.

CHARLIE: What other kind is there?

JOSE: And you've been in love more than three hundred times?

CHARLIE: I fell in love twice this morning, Joey. Look. You fall in love, whaddoes it mean? You'd take a bullet for her? She's all you think about? She makes your

heart beat, makes your cock throb? It's all of the above.
This morning, I step in a bodega—get my cigarettes—
get my coffee—a wintergreen can of Altoids. Young
girl—one a your kind—brown skin, brown eyes—
beautiful—rings me up at the register. Couldn't a been
more'n nineteen. Maybe twenny, twenny one. I give
her the money, she gives me a smile. What'm I thinkin'
about? My phone bill? My fuckin' grandkids? I'm
thinkin' about HER. Heart gets a little boom-boom-
boom, activity begins stirring in the pants—and if some
Dominican motherfucker had walked in there with a
gun? I'd a stepped in front of her and taken one in the
chest. In that moment. Ya understand? People get too,
uh...alright Joey, I'm gonna tell ya somethin'. A little
somethin' I know to be true about love. It's a moment
to moment thing if you want it to be successful. Ya
gotta say to yourself—yes—I am presently enjoying the
company of this lovely young lady by my side. This...
is a good time that I am having—and don't make more
of it than what it is. Start thinkin' 'bout the future?
Start shoppin' out his and hers cemetary plots? This is
not love, Joey. This is a mistake of the delusional. You
enjoy yourself. Ya take it as it comes. Ya grow a little
paunch, get a touch a' gray, start payin' for sex. All a
part a' God's great plan. This *eternal* love crap, Joey. It's
for the fuckin' birds.

Scene 27

(The Bronx Zoo)

*(*VIVIAN, JOHN, *and* JUNIOR *listen to the* ZOO GUIDE *as
she speaks in front of the chimpanzee cage. As she speaks,*
JUNIOR *slowly approaches.)*

ZOO GUIDE: We share over ninety-eight percent of
our genetic make-up with the chimpanzee. More than
ninety-eight percent of our D N A is identical. The

other two percent? What is the other two percent, you may ask?

(ZOO GUIDE *speaks directly to* JUNIOR, *who stands a foot or two away. They lock eyes.*)

ZOO GUIDE: I don't know. I have no idea.

(VIVIAN *and* JOHN *kiss.*)

(*Blackout*)

Scene 28

(GARY's *apartment*)

(JOSE *is on the couch, under a blanket.*)

JOSE: I'm afraid I'm gonna die if I fall asleep.

GARY: That's what I mean about you, bro. Everyone an' their mother wants that they die in their sleep, *you* think about it and it's wallow, fuckin' wallow, woe is me.

JOSE: I miss my wife, Gary.

GARY: If you'd sign the fuckin' divorce papers, you wouldn't have a wife to miss. Now, can I finish my story, please? Okay? So what happened was—every time—rat after rat they'd dump in these buckets a water...

JOSE: ...I DON'T WANNA HEAR ABOUT RATS! I DON'T WANNA HEAR ANOTHER GODDAMN WORD ABOUT RATS!!!

(*Blackout*)

Scene 29

(The Bronx Zoo)

*(*JUNIOR *and* ZOO GUIDE*)*

(Possible, but not necessary: SCIENTISTS *drop rats into glass containers of water. They then place small tree branches into each container.)*

*(*JOHN *and* VIVIAN *are not present.)*

ZOO GUIDE: When rats are placed in buckets of water and given the aid of a small tree branch to hang onto—the rats will last approximately seventeen minutes before tiring, losing their grip and eventually drowning. BUT—if one should choose to SAVE the rats, by removing them from the water prior to the inevitable seventeen minute drowning mark—the next time those rats are dumped in buckets of water, they will hang onto the tree branches for anywhere between twenty-one and twenty-four HOURS. From seventeen MINUTES to twenty plus HOURS—simply by recollecting that HOPE of being saved. Without hope—only death remains.

(The SCIENTISTS *remove the tree branches. The rats drown.)*

(Blackout)

Scene 30

(V A hospital)

*(*JOSE *holds a small invisible body in his arms.)*

DOCTOR KRAMER: Put her down, Jose.

JOSE: She's still breathing.

DOCTOR KRAMER: Put her down.

JOSE: I need to save her.

DOCTOR KRAMER: We're here to save *you*.

JOSE: I have a child of my own.

DOCTOR KRAMER: We're here to make you well.

JOSE: Her blood is on my hands.

DOCTOR KRAMER: We're here to wash them clean.

JOSE: Her intestines are on my uniform.

DOCTOR KRAMER: War is *necessary*, Jose.

JOSE: I need to make things right.

DOCTOR KRAMER: You helped liberate a nation from rape and torture and murder. Where is the wrong in that?

JOSE: Her eyes look like my son's.

DOCTOR KRAMER: You can be both a soldier AND a father.

JOSE: I need money for my boy. I need money for my wife.

DOCTOR KRAMER: We're paying you to rehabilitate.

JOSE: I shut my eyes when I pulled the trigger.

DOCTOR KRAMER: We will make you brave once again.

JOSE: I was never brave.

DOCTOR KRAMER: Seventeen kills is the work of a brave man.

JOSE: Seventeen kills is the work of a murderer.

DOCTOR KRAMER: Not if seventeen thousand have been saved.

JOSE: She stopped breathing—Doctor—Doctor— She stopped breathing.

DOCTOR KRAMER: She's already gone.

JOSE: Her blood is turning black.

DOCTOR KRAMER: Her soul is in a better place.

JOSE: I should've looked where I was shooting.

DOCTOR KRAMER: And lifted your head? And exposed
your body? And risked being shot yourself? What
good would that've done? *(Pause)* Now put her down.
Put her down.

(JOSE gently rests "her" at his feet.)

(JOSE stands and stares straight ahead.)

DOCTOR KRAMER: Good. Very good. Now, how do you
feel? Jose? Tell me how you feel.

(JOSE turns and looks at DOCTOR KRAMER.)

JOSE: I wanna go home.

DOCTOR KRAMER: You are home.

(Blackout)

Scene 31

*(Outside VIVIAN's apartment building. JUNIOR holds a
stuffed blue elephant.)*

JOHN: I enjoyed our kiss earlier.

VIVIAN: I could tell.

JOHN: Yeah. I think you're a really good kisser.

VIVIAN: You do, huh?

JOHN: You probably hear that a lot, though, don't you?

VIVIAN: No, I...

JOHN:...No?

VIVIAN: No.

JOHN: No?

VIVIAN: Not really. No.

(Pause)

JOHN: I see things in you, Vivian.

(Beat)

VIVIAN: Whaddayou see?

(Beat)

JOHN: I see a strength. I see courage. I see an internal beauty to match what I see on the outside.

VIVIAN: ...Please.

JOHN: I do. And I wanna help bring them out in you. I wanna make you smile. Treat you the way you deserve to be treated. Hold your hand and walk in the rain. Take a carriage ride through Central Park in the first winter snow.

VIVIAN: Shut up.

JOHN: That's the smile I'm talkin' about.

VIVIAN: Okay, I get it, I get it...

JOHN: ...Do you? *(Beat)* Do you get it, Vivian?

(Beat)

VIVIAN: I think so.

(Beat)

JOHN: I'd like to take you to dinner tonight. I'd like to take you out dancing. I don't want this day to end. Do you like to dance, Vivian?

VIVIAN: Yeah. And I like dinner too.

(Blackout)

Scene 32

(Barber shop)

(JOSE cuts CHARLIE's hair.)

CHARLIE: Ya look like shit, Joey. Ya know that? Ya look like death warmed over into a boiling pot a' steaming urine. That's not a good look. Edward James Olmos was a hundred an' six an' a fuckin' chain-smoker he'd look better'n you. Ya need to getchyour sleep. Any doctor, any fool, knows ya walk around sleepless ya walk around dead. Have yourself a carrot juice. Celery's supposed to be good. There's a new, uh, whaddaya call it—a juice joint—they got a new juice joint somewhere round here. A juice joint in this neighborhood. Rice and bean smoothies, "Yeah, I'd like a fuckin' cuchifrito protein shake, *por favor.*" I'll give 'em a week til they close—a month an' a half max. But they're open now. Go getchyourself a lil' bee pollen—throw a little Echinacea in it. Join a gym. Check yourself into Bellevue—but getchyour goddamn sleep. Ya walk around with the weight of the world on your shoulders, Joey. It's a nice world, Joey, it really is. Ya just gotta try puttin' it down every once in awhile. Try sharin' it with the rest of us, it's our world, too. I've given you my number before? I'm gonna give you my cell—you're gonna call me when it gets too heavy to carry around all by yourself. We're gonna count to ten together. We'll count to a hundred before we act. Ya keep your nose clean? Ya stay outta trouble, don't run around doin' anything too stupid? Don't make me out an asshole? It's a Louie Armstrong world, son. It's a Louie Armstrong world.

(Blackout)

Scene 33

(VIVIAN's *apartment*)

(JUNIOR *bounces the ball off the wall.*)

(NIKKI *smokes at the kitchen table.*)

NIKKI: *(To offstage)* Maybe he'll bring his handcuffs with him! Shit—he got a friend, or a brother, hook me up—I hook you up—you hook me up—little return a' favor'd be nice.

(VIVIAN *enters in a sexy dress and heels.*)

VIVIAN: I'll be sure to ask. Here—could you help me with this—what time is it?

(NIKKI *zips up the back of* VIVIAN's *dress as:*)

NIKKI: Quarter to—you got fifteen minutes.

VIVIAN: Fifteen minutes. *(Beat)* Alright.

NIKKI: So what's up, what up—he been married, he got kids—what's up with lil' N Y P D?

VIVIAN: No—no wife, no kids— He divorced over ten years ago, he said he wanted kids but his wife didn't, so...that's it—no wife, no kids.

NIKKI: If things work out...maybe he'll get his wish.

VIVIAN: It's a first date, Nik—don't get it twisted.

NIKKI: You never know's all I'm sayin'.

VIVIAN: He's gonna take me to dinner. We're gonna dance a little. That's it. It's a first date. How do I look?

NIKKI: Like a woman who'd like a second date.

VIVIAN: They're always nice in the beginning.

NIKKI: Not some of the motherfuckers I've dated.

VIVIAN: You got anymore cigarettes?

(NIKKI *gives* VIVIAN *a cigarette.*)

VIVIAN: He's nice, Nikki, I dunno. Junior liked him.
He bought him a cotton candy. He got him a stuffed
elephant.

NIKKI: And when I told you he was staring at you
what'd you do? You acted like you weren't interested.

VIVIAN: I don't know if I'm interested now. I'll tell you
by the end of the night.

NIKKI: You'll be on all fours by the end of the night.

VIVIAN: I'm just gonna try to enjoy myself, ya know?
It's been a long time since...He paid me all kinda
compliments and stuff, and...I dunno. I dunno. What
else am I supposed to do? Sit at home with Junior the
rest a my life? Fuckin' hang out with you?

NIKKI: Just try to have fun, alright? Don't think about
it too much. An' forget about that shit I was sayin'
earlier—just try to go an' have a good time.

VIVIAN: Forget about what shit you was sayin' earlier?

NIKKI: About him and, you know, how he could maybe
be Junior's father some day—forget about that shit—
just see what happens, alright? Get outta the house, get
a free meal—go on—You deserve a night every once in
a while. An' that's what you're gonna go have.

VIVIAN: Yeah—I do deserve a night.

NIKKI: That's why I'm sayin' it—you deserve a night—
so—you know, fuckin'...go have one.

VIVIAN: Yeah.

NIKKI: Now go on. Put on some makeup—you got
about twelve minutes.

(Beat)

VIVIAN: (Referring to JUNIOR) Lookit'm.

NIKKI: What?

VIVIAN: Look at him.

NIKKI: Vivian?

VIVIAN: It's bad enough he never SAID nothin'—now he doesn't even LISTEN anymore.

NIKKI: Alright, come on, go get ready—come on.

(Beat)

VIVIAN: *(Re: JOSE)* He useta be a lotta fun, you know?

NIKKI: That was a long time ago, Viv.

VIVIAN: We useta be able to just sit around and do nothing. Nothing but sit around makin' each other laugh.

NIKKI: An' then what happened? Then what?

VIVIAN: He use to sing to me every morning when I woke up.

NIKKI: That's not what I'm talkin' about.

VIVIAN: *(She's deep in it)* Every morning when I woke up he useta sing these old songs in my ear...

NIKKI: ...Here we go...

VIVIAN: ...I remember I'd...I'd tell'm—"Why are you singing that stuff for, baby? That's white people's music. What about Hector Lavoe? What about Willie Colon?" "It ain't white peoples' music," he'd say. "It's lovers' music. Sammy Davis Junior ain't white. Sarah Vaughan ain't white." He wasn't much of a singer, but...it was sweet, ya know? Morning coffee and a serenade. "If I was you, baby...if I was you I'd never be able to do anything with my life. You know why? Cause if I was you I'd never be able to stop looking at myself in the mirror." *(Breaking down)* What do they do to them over there? What the fuck do they do to them? My mom said it was the same with my dad. The same exact shit. What was I supposed to do? There was nothing for me to do. Jesus Christ—lookit me—I'm a fuckin' wreck here. Lookit me. All ready for my big date. All ready to go out dancing.

NIKKI: You look beautiful.

VIVIAN: Why am I even doing this shit? What am I doing? Lookit me.

NIKKI: You look great, okay? Now go on. Splash your face with cold water. If he shows up, I'll stall him til you're done. Now go get ready.

VIVIAN: Tell him I had an emergency.

NIKKI: I ain't tellin'm shit. You said he's a nice guy, he's a nice guy. You had a good time at the zoo. I'm gonna watch Junior for you—and you're gonna stay out as late as you want. Okay? Now go wash your face. Go on. He's a nice guy.

Scene 34

(V A hospital)

(DOCTOR KRAMER sits on one side of a desk. JOSE sits on the other.)

DOCTOR KRAMER: You've been doing a lot of good work, Jose. How do you feel it's been going?

JOSE: I dunno, I...I'm tired, I...I'm really tired.

DOCTOR KRAMER: The human *brain* tries to convince us we *need* sleep—however, medically it's been proven that this isn't the case. There's a man in California—a war hero much like yourself—he hasn't slept in more than twenty-seven years. Sleep is a *want*, Jose, not a need.

JOSE: Yeah, well I want it.

DOCTOR KRAMER: Are you trying to punish yourself by not getting it?

JOSE: I'm not trying to punish myself.

DOCTOR KRAMER: Then why aren't you getting it?
(Beat) Jose.

JOSE: I'm afraid of what I might see. I'm afraid of my thoughts.

DOCTOR KRAMER: Your thoughts are merely synapses firing in your head—they have nothing to do with who you are.

JOSE: They keep me up, though. When I'm at work. When I'm here. When I'm at home, or...at my friend's where I'm stayin' at. All the tests. The training. Work. Too much a'...too much a' everything. I never get a break.

DOCTOR KRAMER: You could quit your job at the barbershop and spend more time here, if you want.

JOSE: No, I need the money.

DOCTOR KRAMER: Maybe we could increase the fee we've been paying you.

JOSE: I just wanna wake up next to my wife again. I wanna be a father to my son. I wanna just...I just wanna go back home. Ya know? I just wanna go home.

(Long pause)

DOCTOR KRAMER: This is nice.

JOSE: What?

DOCTOR KRAMER: This. It...it doesn't feel so... "doctor-patient". It's more like we're just talking. Two men. *(Pause)* I have a wife, Jose. I have three beautiful children. My wife and I have been together for more than *twenty three years*. I know how you feel about your wife. I know how you feel about your little boy. I understand. But as a friend—if I may be frank — your wife doesn't want a husband who's sleeping on a friend's couch. She doesn't want a man who flies

off into fits and episodes and may put her son—your
son—in harm's way. A man who's the wrong kind of
role model. And you've already made a lot of progress,
Jose. Guilt, depression. These are normal feelings upon
one's return. But you've come a long way in a short
period of time. And I think we're gonna be okay. I
think we're just about nearing the top of the hill.

Scene 35

(VIVIAN's *apartment*)

(*The* ZOO GUIDE *and* JUNIOR *smoke cigarettes together.*)

ZOO GUIDE: We make too much of petty things in
this country. Save the whale. Protect the rainforests.
We get our panties in a bunch when a dolphin swims
into a fisherman's net. You can not be inhumane to
something that isn't human. You want to hunt for
deer—hunt for deer. You wanna club a baby seal—
club a baby seal. Eat the brains of a live monkey. It's
delicious. Evolve or die. Charles Darwin and God.
Charles Darwin IS God. It's a taste I've been lucky
enough to enjoy. It's a wonderful taste. And some day,
when you get the chance, I'm quite sure you'll agree.

(*Blackout*)

Scene 36

(GARY's *apartment*)

(GARY *is dressed for a night on the town.* JOSE *is on the
couch.*)

GARY: C'mon man- ya gotta shower an' shit- wash
your hair or somethin'—there's no way you're gettin'
laid lookin' like that. C'mon get dressed. We gotta get
there before nine, bro, or there's a fuckin' cover—and

you know I don't pay no fuckin' cover. C'mon bro—
the fuckin' parade was today—it's gonna be like ASS
heaven tonight. Ass ass ass—everywhere ya look—like
a giant wall a Puerto Rican ass—it's gonna be great,
bro—c'mon I'll buy the first round.

JOSE: I think I'm gonna die.

GARY: You are NOT GONNA FUCKIN' DIE, okay?
You're gonna go out dancing. You're gonna talk to
some women. You're gonna have a few beers. You're
gonna TRY, okay? You're gonna fuckin' TRY—to have
a good time. Now let's get the fuck outta here.

JOSE: I'm tired, man—but I can't fall asleep.

GARY: You can't fall asleep, don't fall asleep—we'll
stay to last call— it's the easiest time to get laid.

JOSE: I'm afraid I'm gonna do something in my dreams
I'm gonna regret.

GARY: I fuck my sister in my dreams!! Who gives a
shit? This shit is driving you fuckin' crazy, bro. Come
on. Let's slam some ass. What's the matter with you?

JOSE: I wanna see my wife.

GARY: Yeah, well, she don't wanna see you. I need a
wing man, bro.

JOSE: I want my wife back, Gary—I don't wanna go an'
fuck some whore.

GARY: You don't wanna go an' fuck some whore.

JOSE: No.

GARY: Alright. Alright. Listen, bro—alright? You know
about Abraham Lincoln an' his wife? Mmmmph? You
know about that shit?

JOSE: Ahh, C-mon, man, I don't wanna hear about
Abraham Lincoln an' his fuckin' wife...

GARY: ...No, no, no—no—listen ta this shit, alright?
Honest Abe had this wife, alright—that he was married
to. Okay? This was the SECOND love of his life—the
FIRST love of his life died when he was like nineteen
or somethin'. Old Abe had a tough time of it from
what I understand. His first love died a' some tragic
something—or—other, his moms died when he was
really young—lotta shit—fuckin' log cabin—but he had
this wife he ended up gettin' married to, okay? And
she was a midget. Okay? A little fuckin' midget. And
ol' Abe? This motherfucker was some'n like...six five,
six-six or some shit—a fuckin' giant, okay? Are you
listening?

JOSE: I'm gonna bring her every cent I've been saving.
I'm goin' over there—I don't care about the restraining
orders—I don't give a shit what she says.

GARY: And thusly the reason for the restraining order
in the first place. Now lemme finish my goddamn
story, alright? Now listen carefully to this shit. Okay.
So—ol' Abe—Abraham-fuckin'-six-foot-six-born
in a log cabin motherfucker—this goofy-bearded
motherfucker marries a midget woman no taller than
this big—this fuckin' high she was—like a half-a-
midget. And she useta beat the shit outta him. Alright?
The fuckin' midget would BEAT THE LIVIN' SHIT
outta her husband—and what husband was that, Jose?
Joe Blow? Ordinary Schmo? Guy like you or me? No!
This was ABRAHAM LINCOLN. She'd beat the shit
outta Abraham fuckin' Lincoln. The lil' midget. Fuckin'
guy could free an entire peoples of the horrors of
fuckin' slavery- he could not control his own lil' midget
wife. That's all I'm sayin'. Now come on. It's ass time.

Scene 37

(Club San Juan. A salsa club.)

(JOHN and VIVIAN dance. They make great partners. They dance and dance and dance.)

(GARY enters and makes his move on a woman— unsuccessfully. He begins to dance off after her, moving offstage.)

(We then find JOSE, standing frozen. His eyes glued on JOHN and VIVIAN.)

(JOHN and VIVIAN's dance grows in its eroticism. It is animal and sexual and erotic and beautiful. They are swept up in the magic of the moment.)

(The salsa music fades to silence. They dance to no music.)

(JOSE begins to sing I Get Along Without You.*)*

JOSE: *(Singing)* I get along without you very well
Of course I do
Except when soft rains fall
And drip from leaves
Then I recall the thrill of being sheltered
In your arms
Of course I do
But I get along without you very well.

(Silence)

(JOSE continues to stare. JOHN and VIVIAN continue to dance.)

(The salsa music slowly rises and rises and rises and rises and rises. JOSE covers his ears.)

(Blackout/silence)

END OF ACT ONE

ACT TWO

Scene 1

(JUNIOR, *in his pajamas, sits alone on stage—holding his little blue ball. We begin to hear.*)

JOHN: *(V O)* Mmm, ya like that don't you?

VIVIAN: *(V O)* Maybe.

JOHN: *(V O)* How 'bout this? You like this, too?

VIVIAN: *(V O)* Who wants to know?

(JOHN *and* VIVIAN's *elongated shadows appear on the back wall.* JOHN *unzips the back of her dress.*)

JOHN: Mmm—You're a lil' wildcat.

VIVIAN: Meow.

(*The dress falls to the floor. She turns. They kiss.*)

JOHN: Wildcat. You're a fuckin' animal.

VIVIAN: ROAR!

(*Center stage, lights up on* JOSE—*inside a giant container of water. He struggles to get out. He struggles to reach* VIVIAN.)

(JOHN *turns* VIVIAN *around and holds her arms behind her back.*)

JOHN: Oh yeah—you like it rough, don't you? Tell me how much you like it.

VIVIAN: Oww.

JOHN: How 'bout this? This feel good?

VIVIAN: John.

JOHN: Taken from behind over your own kitchen table.

(JOHN *bends* VIVIAN *over the table.*)

VIVIAN: Shit.

JOHN: Wildcat.

(*Lights up on the* ZOO GUIDE—*between the giant rat tank and* JOHN/VIVIAN.)

ZOO GUIDE: Notice how they struggle for contact. How they yearn for something to grab hold of that is just out of reach.

JOHN: Just the way you like it.

VIVIAN: Please.

ZOO GUIDE: How they struggle and fight. How they claw and kick and scream.

VIVIAN: John.

JOHN: Meow.

ZOO GUIDE: But with no help, there can be no hope. Hopelessness is helplessness. Helplessness is hopelessness. Survival will last for seventeen minutes.

(JOSE *struggles to get out of the tank. He struggles to not drown. He struggles to reach* VIVIAN. JOHN *thrusts* VIVIAN *from behind.* JUNIOR *holds his little blue ball and stares at the* ZOO GUIDE. *The* ZOO GUIDE *stares at* JUNIOR.)

(*A single light reveals* CHARLIE—*sitting in the barber's chair, reading the* New York Post.)

CHARLIE: (*Sings*)
I hear babies cry,
I watch them grow,
They'll learn much more than I'll ever know.
And I think to myself:

What a wonderful world,
Yes, I think to myself
What a wonderful world...

(The struggles continue. JUNIOR *and the* ZOO GUIDE *continue to stare.* CHARLIE *puts down the paper and stares out into the audience. Five seconds)*

(Blackout)

Scene 2

(V A hospital)

JOSE: I need to see Doctor Kramer.

RECEPTIONIST: Our business hours are over.

JOSE: I need to see my doctor!

RECEPTIONIST: The doctors will be in tomorrow morning.

JOSE: I NEED TO SEE MY FUCKIN' DOCTOR!!!

(Blackout)

Scene 3

(VIVIAN's apartment)

(JUNIOR, on the floor in his pajamas, bounces his little blue ball.)

(JOHN smokes at the kitchen table.)

(Lights remain on JUNIOR and JOHN as:)

(Lights up on JOSE at the payphone, a small piece of paper in his hand as he dials.)

JOSE: Hello, Charlie? Charlie, it's me, Jose. Jose. Joey from the barbershop. I'm not too good, Charlie, I... the weight of the world, Charlie...I was wondering if

I could maybe give you some of it. I've COUNTED to
ten—I've *counted* to a *hundred*—I need something more,
I...ya think there's anyway I could maybe see you right
now, I...Oh. Okay. Okay. I'll call you some other time.

(Lights out on JOSE.*)*

(Lights remain on JUNIOR *and* JOHN.*)*

(Lights up on CHARLIE *in the barber chair.)*

CHARLIE: It's a nice world—if ya want it ta be. It's a
Louie Armstrong world. Ain't a bad place to live. Not
too bad. Gotta relax. Can't let it get to ya. Gotta learn to
ignore it.

(Lights out on CHARLIE*)*

(Lights remain on JUNIOR *and* JOHN. *The phone begins to
ring.)*

(Lights up on JOSE, *receiver to his ear. Ring, ring, ring, as:)*

JOSE: Love and love and love and...

*(*JOSE *SLAMS and SLAMS and SLAMS the receiver against
its cradle as the phone stops ringing and:)*

JOSE: ...AND LOVE AND LOVE AND LOVE AND
LOVE AND LOVE!!!

(Lights out on JOSE.*)*

(LIGHTS remain on JUNIOR *and* JOHN.*)*

*(*JOHN *puts out his cigarette and moves toward the front
door.)*

*(*JUNIOR *intentionally doesn't catch the ball and lets it roll
toward* JOHN. JOHN *picks it up.)*

*(*JUNIOR *doesn't turn around to face* JOHN.*)*

JOHN: You want me to toss it back to you? Mmmph?
Yes? No? I'll keep it myself if you don't say anything.
Okay, then...don't say I didn't warn you.

*(*JUNIOR *turns to face* JOHN. JUNIOR *puts his hands out.)*

JOHN: Let's see what kinda hands you got.

(JOHN *softly lobs the ball to* JUNIOR. JUNIOR *catches it.*)

JOHN: Well...alright, then.

(JUNIOR *throws it back to* JOHN, *who catches it.*)

JOHN: Nice throw.

(JOHN *throws it back.* JUNIOR *catches it.* VIVIAN *enters in her bathrobe. Her eyes are red and wet. She stares at* JOHN.)

(Pause)

JOHN: I'm gonna go now. *(Beat)* Maybe I'll see you again sometime. *(Beat)* I'd like that. *(He exits.)*

(VIVIAN *looks at* JUNIOR. JUNIOR *looks at* VIVIAN.)

(VIVIAN *slowly lifts and extends her hands out toward* JUNIOR—*in an attempt to play catch. He continues to hold the ball.*)

(Blackout)

Scene 4

(JOSE *runs in place.*)

JOSE: Lightning splits my head wide open
Bathing me in blood and sorrow
Existence now behind me
Releasing me in death
A wedding altar drenched in blood
Me with hers and her with mine
Mustard gas and napalm
Dynamite and school buses
Gas masks and MOPP suits
Sandstorms and firestorms
Hand grenades and car bombs
America and love.

(Blackout)

Scene 5

(VIVIAN's *apartment*)

(VIVIAN *sits at the kitchen table, staring blankly at a cup of tea.*)

(JUNIOR *is on the floor bouncing his little blue ball against the wall.*)

(*Sammy Davis Jr sings "Blame it on My Youth"— beginning with the lyrics: "If I expected love when first we kissed."*)

(*Fifteen seconds*)

(*Fade to black*)

Scene 6

(*V A hospital*)

(DOCTOR KRAMER *is on his side of the desk.*)

(JOSE *manically paces about the other side.*)

JOSE: ...And I couldn't move, I stood there, I stood and stared and stood and stared and stood and stared and wanted to kill her and wanted to kiss her and wanted to throw myself at her feet and wanted to grab him by the throat and bite his fuckin' tongue out and beg for her forgiveness and stick a k-bar in his heart, an M-60 up her ass and hold her and kiss her and lift her in my arms and carry her over the threshold and make love to every cell of her body and fuck her with my soul and cry every tear I ever cried and bathe her in my tears and baptize her with my blood and spit and piss and shit and cum and I stood and stared and stood and stared and you were nowhere to be found, oil and blood and death and sand fuckin' me in my guts and my mind and I thought I was okay, I thought I was gettin' better, I was makin' progress, I was becoming

the man you promised me you'd make me, the soldier
with the brave heart, the soldier who did good before
and would do good again and would hold her in his
arms and would tell her that he loved her and I stood
and stared and stood and stared and said nothing and
did nothing and watched her disappear in the arms of
another as the child I've always been told me fuck you
Jose—you ain't good enough, Jose—fuck you Jose—
you ain't smart enough, Jose—fuck you Jose—you're a
murderer, Jose—fuck you Jose, fuck you!—she didn't
want you since the beginning—you're a child, Jose—
you're an infant and a baby, you're a liar and a loser
and a coward and I was making progress, Doctor. I
was getting better. I've been doing everything I know
how. I've done everything you asked me to do. And
I stood and stared. I stood there and I stared and
said nothing. And where were YOU!? Where WERE
you, Doctor? I needed to see you. I needed to talk to
you. But you were nowhere to be found. (In tears and
exhausted, he has collapsed into his chair across the desk
from DOCTOR KRAMER.) You were nowhere to be found,
Doctor. Where were you?

DOCTOR KRAMER: I'm right here.

(Blackout)

Scene 7

(VIVIAN's apartment)

(VIVIAN is still seated at the kitchen table. Sammy Davis Jr
sings.)

(The ZOO GUIDE enters and faces JUNIOR. She puts her
arms out—as VIVIAN had done earlier.)

(JUNIOR tosses her the ball. She tosses it back.)

(Toss—catch—)

(Toss—catch—)

(Toss—catch—)

*(Z*OO G*UIDE slowly exits.)*

*(V*IVIAN *and* J*UNIOR remain.)*

(Silence)

(Slow fade to black)

Scene 8

(V A hospital)

*(*DOCTOR KRAMER*'s on his side of the desk,* JOSE*'s on his. He is calm. He has settled down.)*

DOCTOR KRAMER: You did the right thing, Jose.

JOSE: I didn't do anything.

DOCTOR KRAMER: You *did* do something. You controlled yourself. *(Beat)* Did she see you?

JOSE: No.

DOCTOR KRAMER: That's good, too. You don't want her to see you for the first time out at a single's club, do you? In a world where it would appear that you have forgotten her and moved on?

JOSE: That's the way I saw her.

DOCTOR KRAMER: You're trying to get HER back—not the other way around. You did the right thing, Jose. The first time she sees you again—she should see you as the man she wants to share her life with.

JOSE: And what if I can't be that?

DOCTOR KRAMER: You already are. You're more than that. You're a soldier, Jose.

JOSE: That's why she left me in the first place.

DOCTOR KRAMER: She left you for being a soldier?
Or she left you for bringing the war back to your
apartment with you? Jose. Before we started working
together—if you had seen your wife at that nightclub—
would you have done something right now you'd be
sitting here regretting? Would you have exhibited the
sort of discipline and restraint of the American soldier,
the way you did? Or would you have behaved like a
child unable to exist in the world? SHE didn't desert
the soldier—YOU did.

JOSE: I killed innocent people.

DOCTOR KRAMER: To free millions of others.

JOSE: Yeah, but now I'm the one's gotta live with it, not
you.

DOCTOR KRAMER: That's right—you do and I don't.
But you also GET to live with the millions you SAVED.
And FREED. And I don't get to do that either. I wish
I did, but I don't. Let me ask you a question, Jose. Do
you place more value on the life of the individual—
over the nation of people in which that individual
may live? Mmmph? Are you a man who cares about
the wives of the world, or only about *your own* wife?
Are you a man who cares about the children of the
world, or only about your *own* child? I'm asking you a
question, Jose—do you care about the others?

JOSE: Yeah, of course.

DOCTOR KRAMER: And do you think that's a bad thing?
To care about ALL PEOPLE EQUALLY? Do you think
your WIFE thinks that's a bad thing? Do you really
believe that's why she's turned her back on you? Is
that what you believe, Jose? Or is that just what you
want to blame—instead of taking responsibility for
your own weaknesses and inabilities to live with the
good that you have done? These are good qualities—
selflessness and bravery and discipline and honor and

patriotism. These are qualities that any woman would
love to have in her man. Do you believe in democracy,
Jose? Mmmph? Do you cherish your freedom to
worship as you choose? Your freedom to speak your
mind when and where you want to speak it? Your
freedom to eat what you want, and wear what you
want, and live where you want and LOVE who you
want? Do you? Do you believe these are good things,
these small freedoms that we as Americans possess?
Answer me—yes or no.

JOSE: Yeah, I...

DOCTOR KRAMER: ...And how about for others
throughout the rest of the world? Do you feel that
women should be able to vote or get an education?
Do you feel children around the world, like your son,
should be allowed to become doctors or lawyers or
stock brokers if this is what they aspire to become? Yes
or no? Yes or no, Jose?

JOSE: Yes.

DOCTOR KRAMER: Yes. I feel the same way. But doctors
won't make this a reality. Or lawyers. Or stock brokers.
Or barbers or hot dog vendors. Soldiers will, Jose.
In fact—you've already played a small part in that,
haven't you? Your sacrifices, your selflessness, your
bravery—these things already HAVE—and hopefully
will continue—to bring these freedoms to those less
fortunate than we are here in America. It's men like
you, Jose—SOLDIERS like you—that can make this a
reality for the rest of the world. Do you believe these
freedoms are important enough to be fighting for? Yes
or no?

JOSE: Yes sir.

DOCTOR KRAMER: So do I. How about dying for? Are
these freedoms important enough to die for, Jose? A
few people for the benefit of millions? Yes or no?

JOSE: Yes sir.

DOCTOR KRAMER: And what about killing for?

JOSE: Yes sir.

DOCTOR KRAMER: Yes. I agree with you. I couldn't agree with you more soldier.

(Blackout)

Scene 9

(VIVIAN's apartment)

(JUNIOR is on the floor in his pajamas holding his little blue ball.)

(We hear the ZOO GUIDE, but do not see her.)

ZOO GUIDE: *(V O)*Survival of the fittest. Evolve or die. The natural pecking order of the world. The great food chain working to perfection. Charles Darwin and God. Charles Darwin IS God.

(Blackout)

Scene 10

(V A hospital)

(JOSE runs on the treadmill. NURSES record his vital signs. DOCTOR KRAMER holds up one Rorschach card after another.)

JOSE: The American flag. Stars and stripes. The Vietnam Memorial. The Tomb of the Unknown Soldier. The Washington Monument. Arlington Cemetary. Capitol Hill.

DOCTOR KRAMER: Good.

JOSE: Normandy. Baghdad. Pearl Harbor.

DOCTOR KRAMER: ...Good. Faster...

JOSE: ...Valley Forge. Gettysburg. Independance Hall. Korea...

DOCTOR KRAMER: ...Faster...

JOSE: ...The Liberty Bell. Mount Rushmore...

DOCTOR KRAMER: ...Faster...

JOSE: ...Paul Revere. George Washington. Ulysses S. Grant. Francis Scott Key...

DOCTOR KRAMER: ...Faster...

JOSE: ...Appomattux. Crispus Attucks...

DOCTOR KRAMER: ...Faster...

JOSE: ...Audie Murphy—Hiroshima—Nagasaki.

DOCTOR KRAMER: ...Good, faster...

JOSE: ...Mussolini— Hitler—Saddam —Osama...

DOCTOR KRAMER: ...GOOD!...

JOSE: ...Democracy...

DOCTOR KRAMER: ...YES!...

JOSE: ...Liberty...

DOCTOR KRAMER: ...YES!...

JOSE: ...America...

DOCTOR KRAMER: ...Faster...

JOSE: ...America...

DOCTOR KRAMER: ...YES!...

JOSE: ...America...

DOCTOR KRAMER: ...Faster...

JOSE: ...America...

DOCTOR KRAMER: ...YES!!!...

JOSE: ...America!!!...

(Blackout)

(Emergency sirens blare. Glass breaks. Horns honk. Search lights swirl. Firecrackers explode. Fires burn. Helicopters fly overhead. CHAOS. CONFUSION.)

Scene 11

(GARY's apartment)

(The stage is black with the exception of the light from an occasional firework or siren outside the window. The chaos outside continues.)

(In the occasional light we make out JOSE putting on his camouflage military fatigues. Eventually:)

(The door opens with a drunken burst and the flood of a high-powered flashlight. It is GARY and the ZOO GUIDE.)

GARY: I'm gonna tap that ass, tap that ass.

ZOO GUIDE: I'm gonna tap yours bitch.

GARY: You gonna be walkin' bow-legged for the next week an' a half.

(The flashlight shines on JOSE.)

GARY: Whoa—what's up with the costume, bro?

JOSE: I'm gonna go check on Vivian and Junior. I wanna make sure they're okay with the blackout.

GARY: Okay with the blackout? What're ya fuckin' kiddin' me? Bro- you gotta check it out bro—fuckin' incredible out there—fuckin' unbelievable—LOOK— LOOK—Jose—this is Linda. Linda—this is Jose. Jose, Linda, Linda, Jose. It's been a good day, bro.

JOSE: How you doin' Linda?

LINDA: How you doin', soldier boy?

JOSE: I'm doin' great, thanks.

GARY: Yo, bro—this is the shit I been talkin' 'bout,
bro—I met her at the ZOO an' shit—fuckin' Zoo Guide
givin' a tour an' shit—we make eye contact, okay?
So I'm like—fuck it—I step to her—start talkin' shit,
bro—makin' conversation—CONVERSATION—I tell'r
about the rats, okay? THE FUCKIN' DROWNIN' RAT
DOCUMENTARY! She got that shit on TAPE, bro!
Fuckin' chemistry, bro! We end up suckin' down beers
she gets off work in the friendly zoo beer garden—
fuckin' BLACKOUT—NOTHIN'—end up walkin'
home together from the fuckin' BRONX, bro—BX
in the mothafuckin' HOUSE—it's like the end a' the
world out there, bro—fuckin' bedlam—this is what I
been talkin' about—nobody's out there thinkin' 'bout
nothin'—they're just doin' the shit—drinkin' in the
streets—hangin' out trunks a' cars—walkin' 'round
fuckin' NAKED, bro—NAKED! You gotta get out
there bro, I'm tellin' ya, shit's like, fuckin'...I don't even
know, bro—it's a night ta fuckin' remember an' shit!
Ain't that right, Lovely Linda?

LINDA: That's right, uh...what's your name again?

GARY: What's my...GARY, sweetface, fuck'samatter
wi'choo?

LINDA: That's right—Gorgeous Gary.

GARY: You hear that shit, bro? Gorgeous Gary she calls
me.

JOSE: *(Trying to leave)* It was nice to meet you, Linda. I
need to go check on my wife now.

GARY: Hold up, bro—c'mon—fuckin' watch this shit
alright? Linda here can make the exact same sound as
a fuckin' monkey gettin' its brains eatin' up an' shit—
funny shit, bro, lighten your shit up a little—Show'm
that shit Lovely Linda.

LINDA: Why don't you do it for him instead, Gorgeous?

JOSE: *(Heading for the door)* Maybe some other time.

GARY: *(Blocking his path)* Whoa, whoa, whoa, whoa, whoa—wait up, bro—alright—I'll show ya the shit, okay?—prolly ain't funny as this bitch, cuz this bitch like high fuckin' comedy she do that shit, but, okay— lend me a hand, sweetface—*Gorillas in the Mist* an' shit.

(GARY holds his head as if in a vice and imitates the death cry of a wailing monkey as ZOO GUIDE pretends to eat his brains.)

GARY: Delicious, bro—ya want some? Fuckin' delicacy de la cabeza. *(He begins the death cry once again. Laughing, wailing—ridiculousness.)*

(JOSE exits.)

(ZOO GUIDE stops eating and puts her hands over GARY's hands—tightening the vice around his head.)

ZOO GUIDE: Do you eat pussy like I eat brains, Gary?

GARY: I'm gonna eatchyour ass too, sweetface.

ZOO GUIDE: You're gonna do whatever I want—You're my little monkey-bitch. *(She squeezes with even greater force.)*

GARY: I'm your little monkey man.

ZOO GUIDE: You're my fuckin' whore!

GARY: Tell me you're my sister—tell me you're my fuckin' sister!!!

(Blackout)

(The exterior chaos grows to previously unreached proportions.)

(Eventually, it fades to complete silence.)

(More silence)

(Then:)

Scene 12

(VIVIAN's *apartment*)

(*The entire stage is now her apartment.*)

(*Burning candles fill the stage. Fifty, sixty, seventy candles burn.*)

(VIVIAN *and* JOSE *face each other in the doorway.*)

(JOSE *is in his fatigues.*)

(JOSE *holds out a wad of cash.*)

JOSE: I brought you money, Vivian. I've been working real hard. I've been tryin' real hard to become the man you want me to be. I've been workin' real hard to become a father to my son. (*Pause*) Can I see him, Vivian? Can I come in and see my son?

VIVIAN: He's sleeping.

JOSE: I'd like you to take the money. I've worked real hard to save it up for the two of you. Please.

(VIVIAN *takes the money.*)

VIVIAN: Thank you.

JOSE: It's not as much as I woulda liked. Next time I'll try to bring you more.

VIVIAN: You're not supposed to be here.

JOSE: I know. But the blackout, Vivian. I wanted to make sure you were alright.

VIVIAN: I'm fine.

JOSE: And our son. I wanted to make sure our son was okay.

VIVIAN: We both are.

JOSE: It's a scary time out there, Vivian. You can't see the world for what it is.

VIVIAN: There are orders from the court.

JOSE: I know. I know. I tried to call first, but...I couldn't get through. I got worried. I try to call a lot actually. Nobody ever picks up the phone.

VIVIAN: Thank you for checking up on us.

JOSE: I've been going to a lot of therapy lately, you know, um...I've been feeling a lot better about things. About us. I've been doing okay, I...I've been doin' real good, I...I'm feeling a lot better about myself. How are you, Vivian? You're as pretty as the day we first met. I think you're even prettier to tell you the truth.

VIVIAN: You look good, too.

JOSE: I've been trying to take care of myself, ya know? Tryin' to take responsibility, just...you know...tryin' real hard to let you see I'm ready to come back home.

VIVIAN: Jose...

JOSE: ...Ya know—when I dug out my uniform I found this letter. In the pocket. I, um...there's a lotta things in it that, well, maybe I didn't send it cuz I wasn't ready to, ya know? But...I could read it to you now, if that's alright.

VIVIAN: Why don't you just leave it with me?

JOSE: I'd kinda like to be here when you read it, you know—if you won't let me read it to you myself. I'm kinda nervous a little right now. There's so much I wanna say. There's so much I need to apologize for and...and I, um...well...

(JOSE *opens the letter.*)

VIVIAN: It's late.

JOSE: I know, let me just...it took a lot for me to come here.

VIVIAN: Jose.

JOSE: *(Reads)* "My Dear Vivian—My Love—I write to
you this lonely night here in Iraq. I haven't slept in
more than three days. I try to steal an hour here, ten
minutes there, hoping to fall asleep and be with you
in my dreams. But I am too tired to sleep. I am too
afraid. So I daydream about you instead. I find myself
constantly daydreaming about once again kissing your
sweet face. Your face and your eyes. They make me
feel safe, Vivian. When the bullets are flying and the
explosions and fires are all around me—I try to think
of your face and your eyes. That makes me feel better.
When I get back I want to take you to nice restaurants
where people wear dresses and suits and ties. I'm sorry
we didn't do more of that before I left. If I get back
safe, I promise you we will. I want to buy you jewelry
and fur coats and diamond rings. If I get back maybe
I could even buy you a new wedding ring instead of
that little one I got you. Maybe we could even re-new
our vows and have a bigger wedding and reception
and invite all the people we couldn't afford to invite
the first time, and all the people we've met since. And
Junior could be the one that carries the ring down the
aisle all dressed up in a little tuxedo with a bow-tie.
And we could write our own vows this time instead
of just what the priest told us to say. Or if you don't
want to, I hope it will be okay if I do, so I can tell you
how much I love you in front of everyone we know.
We could even invite strangers off the street so as
many people as possible will know how much I love
you. We could do it in Central Park or in Times Square
and I could shout my vows through a megaphone so
everybody in the world will know exactly how I feel.
Or I could just whisper softly in your ear so it would
be our secret and nobody else's. There are so many
things I want to do when I get back if I don't get killed
while I'm here. Everyday it seems another friend gets
killed or kills himself. There is so much death and, I

don't know why, but I think I might die too. I probably deserve it because of the terrible things I've done here and to you and Junior. If there was only a way that I could take it all back—the way I'd cry myself to sleep in your arms. And the way I always needed you to be there for me to listen to my problems or understand my anger, but didn't listen enough to you. And how I left Junior to you to raise instead of trying to help you with that. I know I've told you I'd change before but I never did. I will now if I make it out of here alive. I will make up for everything, Vivian. I won't TRY, I won't make promises—I'll just do it. And if you could only forgive me for even half of the mistakes that I've made then I could maybe go to sleep now and not be afraid that a bullet or a bomb might kill me tonight in my sleep. If you could forgive me for even half, I would take the bullet happily, knowing that you won't hate me when I'm gone. And when Junior has nightmares or tears and you hold him in your arms to comfort him a little, maybe you could think of me a little bit too. And when he says his first word I hope that word is Mommy. Or Mom. And I hope he says it with the same love that I feel when I say the word Vivian. You are my heart, my love. You are my angel. You have given me reason to breathe. You are the ONLY reason I breathe. You and Junior. And if when this letter finds you I am no longer breathing, please Vivian, please KNOW, my last breath was taken with your name on my tongue. Yours in life. Yours in death. Yours always. Jose.

(JOSE *holds out the letter.* VIVIAN *doesn't take it. Long pause*)

VIVIAN: I don't hate you, Jose.

(*Long pause*)

JOSE: Could I just, um...could I just sneak a quick peek at him? Just...just so I can see him.

VIVIAN: Another time.

JOSE: Please. *(Beat)* Let me see my son. And then I promise I'll leave.

(VIVIAN hesitates and then moves to the side. JOSE enters and puts the letter on the kitchen table. He picks up a long white candle and moves for the bedroom.)

(VIVIAN lights a cigarette.)

(Eventually, JOSE re-enters, candle in hand.)

JOSE: He's sweating in his sleep. The poor. We're like that. Either we can't sleep, or when we do, we seem to sweat a lot. Have you noticed that? I have. *(Long pause. He takes in the apartment. He moves to the kitchen table. Pause)* Is this where he stood...my love?

VIVIAN: I don't know what you're talking about.

JOSE: You were supposed to be the good in the world. You wore white at our wedding.

VIVIAN: You promised you'd leave after you saw him.

JOSE: YOU WORE WHITE AT OUR WEDDING!

VIVIAN: I don't wanna call the police.

JOSE: The phones are dead. *(Pause)* Did our son sleep on the couch while they had you in our bed? I asked you a fuckin' question!!

VIVIAN: I'm gettin' the cops.

(VIVIAN moves for the door—JOSE knocks her to the ground.)

JOSE: Did they have you in our bed! In our bed! Answer me! Did they FUCK YOU in our bed?! Where did they fuck you Vivian?! Where did they fuck you? *(Beat)* ANSWER ME!! *(Beat)* I saw him with you. His paws all over you. Dancing in public. Dancing to embarrass me. IN PUBLIC VIVIAN! How many? How many others have there been?!

VIVIAN: What did they do to you?

JOSE: ANSWER MY GODDAMN QUESTION!!

VIVIAN: I don't know who you are.

JOSE: Private First Class, Jose Solo, sir—reporting for duty, sir!

VIVIAN: Jose, please...

JOSE: You are my wife!

VIVIAN: Not anymore.

(JOSE *hits her.*)

JOSE: You will always be my wife!

VIVIAN: It's over.

(JOSE *hits* VIVIAN *again.*)

JOSE: I am your goddamn HUSBAND!!

VIVIAN: Leave me alone.

JOSE: You were supposed to be the good in the world.

VIVIAN: I wanna be left alone.

JOSE: The world has soiled your beauty.

VIVIAN: It soiled yours.

JOSE: I am a child of God.

VIVIAN: Please.

JOSE: Every boy needs his daddy.

VIVIAN: No he doesn't!

JOSE: Someone who teaches him right from wrong.

(VIVIAN *pulls out divorce papers and slams them on the kitchen table as:*)

VIVIAN: Jose!

JOSE: Someone who'll protect him from the world.

(VIVIAN *holds out a pen as:*)

VIVIAN: It's over.

JOSE: Someone to protect him from people like you.

VIVIAN: Jose!

JOSE: You used to be so beautiful.

VIVIAN: It's over.

JOSE: Pure as diamonds. Pure as love

(VIVIAN *continues to hold the pen in his direction. She is strong. She's determined. Her words are clear and precise.*)

VIVIAN: It's over.

(Pause)

JOSE: I understand. Yes. I understand. *(He takes the pen.)* Pure as love.

(As JOSE *signs,* VIVIAN *turns away.)*

JOSE: Pure as murder.

(JOSE *quickly stabs* VIVIAN *in her neck with the pen. He speaks calmly, methodically.*)

JOSE: I understand.

(JOSE *stabs* VIVIAN *again.*)

JOSE: Pure as death.

(JOSE *stabs* VIVIAN *again.*)

(He holds her limp body in his arms.)

JOSE: I understand. Yes. I understand.

(Blood is spattered everywhere. JOSE *kisses* VIVIAN *on the cheek.)*

JOSE: It's okay now. Everything's okay.

(JOSE *stabs* VIVIAN *once more. He gently moves to the ground—holding her in his arms, stroking her hair, speaking to her as she fades away and dies.*)

JOSE: Sshh. Sshh. It's okay. It's okay. Sshh. That's it.
That's it. Time to sleep, my angel. Time to finally sleep.

(JOSE *rests his head on* VIVIAN's *chest and closes his eyes.
The candles continue to burn.*)

(*Time passes.*)

(*The dawn sun breaks through the windows.*)

(JUNIOR, *in his pajamas, enters from the bedroom.*)

(JUNIOR *stands above* JOSE *and* VIVIAN, *who lie in a large
pool of blood.*)

(*Silence*)

(JUNIOR *takes his usual place on the floor and begins to
bounce his blue rubber ball against the wall.*)

(JOSE *stirs awake.* JUNIOR *continues with the ball.*)

(JOSE *takes off his coat and places it over* VIVIAN's *dead
body.*)

(*One by one he gently blows out the candles.*)

(*He goes to the phone on the wall and picks it up. He pulls a
piece of paper out of his pocket and looks at it. He dials.*)

JOSE: (*Into phone*) Hello, Charlie? It's Joey from the
barber shop. Yeah, yeah, I...I know you must be
extremely busy, but, uh...I messed up pretty bad,
Charlie. Yeah, real bad. I think I'm gonna need your
help. Yeah, if you could, I... I'd appreciate it. Yeah,
okay, I'm...I'm at, uh 2-2-7...2-2-7 116th Street. Offa
Lenox... Number 2-F. Yeah, F. Thanks, Charlie.

(JOSE *hangs up. His bloody handprint on the phone. He tries
to look at* JUNIOR, *but he can't. He stares at* VIVIAN's *body
and blood.*)

(JUNIOR *continues with the ball.*)

(*Silence*)

JOSE: *(With great difficulty)* If you don't wanna talk to me, you don't have to. *(Pause)* I'm not gonna tell you what you should do. Good parents shouldn't tell their children what they should do. *(Pause)* You can do whatever you want. *(Pause)* So long as you're happy. So long as you remember to count to a hundred before you do it. *(pause)* You're not me. *(Pause)* You're not your mother. *(Pause)* I need you to remember that.

(JUNIOR continues with the ball.)

(The front door, which is slightly ajar already, is pushed open.)

(CHARLIE, in uniform, enters.)

JOSE: Thanks for coming, Charlie.

CHARLIE: Jesus.

JOSE: I'm glad it's gonna be you that takes me in.

CHARLIE: Me too.

JOSE: I hope I didn't make you an asshole on this, Charlie. I'm sorry if I caused you any trouble.

CHARLIE: No.

JOSE: It's a Louie Armstrong world, son. I need you to remember that, too. Isn't that right, Charlie? It's a Louie Armstrong world.

CHARLIE: Yeah. If you want it to be.

JOSE: Yeah. Okay, then. Okay. I'm gonna go now son. You take care of yourself, okay? *(Pause)* Okay.

(JOSE moves toward CHARLIE.)

JOSE: We did some good, right Charlie? We did some good?

CHARLIE: Yeah.

JOSE: I got too many emotions, Charlie. They get to me sometimes.

CHARLIE: It's okay.

JOSE: Yeah. I'm gonna be okay. Okay, then.

(JOSE *puts his hands behind his back and turns his back to* CHARLIE.)

JOSE: *(Re: The handcuffs)* Okay.

(CHARLIE *cuffs* JOSE.)

(Before they can leave...)

JUNIOR: And then the three of us can crawl into bed together—and we can rent old black and white movies and order Chinese food or pizza for delivery. Not the black and white movies with Humphrey Bogart or James Cagney with all the violence in them—but something nice for Junior to see. What's the one about Santa Claus and the little girl where nobody really believes he's Santa Claus except for her? That would be a good one for us to watch. It's a good movie. It's about believing in things even when everybody else tries to make it so you don't believe in them. If you believe hard enough in something, there is no such thing as hoping against hope. It's like love. If you believe in it hard enough—no matter what might happen or what people might think about it -- love lasts forever if you want it to. At least that's what I believe anyway. I love you Vivian. I love you too Junior. I can't wait to see you both soon. You are the reasons why I try to stay alive.

(The lights slowly fade to black.)

END OF PLAY

www.ingramcontent.com/pod-product-compliance
Lightning Source LLC
Chambersburg PA
CBHW052215090426
42741CB00010B/2549